S0-AAC-291

Syrian Heritage

Celebrating Diversity in My Classroom

By Tamra B. Orr

21st Century
Junior Library

Published in the United States of America by
Cherry Lake Publishing
Ann Arbor, Michigan
www.cherrylakepublishing.com

Reading Adviser: Cecilia Minden, PhD, Literacy expert and children's author

Photo Credits: ©Zdenek Chaloupka/Shutterstock, cover; ©Waj/Shutterstock, 4; ©ESB Professional/
Shutterstock, 6; ©OBJM/Shutterstock, 8; ©leolintang/Shutterstock, 10; ©Peter Hermes Furian/
Shutterstock, 12; ©Zurijeta/Shutterstock, 14; ©Rus S/Shutterstock, 16; ©Anton Chalakov/Thinkstock, 18;
©Prazis Images/Shutterstock, 20

Library of Congress Cataloging-in-Publication Data
Name: Orr, Tamra, author.
Title: Syrian heritage / Tamra B. Orr.
Description: Ann Arbor : Cherry Lake Publishing, 2018. | Series: Celebrating diversity in my classroom |
    Includes bibliographical references and index.
Identifiers: LCCN 2018003323 | ISBN 9781534129078 (hardcover) | ISBN 9781534132276 (pbk.) |
    ISBN 9781534130777 (pdf) | ISBN 9781534133976 (hosted ebook)
Subjects: LCSH: Syria—Juvenile literature. | Syria—Social life and customs—Juvenile literature.
Classification: LCC DS93 .O77 2018 | DDC 956.91—dc23
LC record available at https://lccn.loc.gov/2018003323

Cherry Lake Publishing would like to acknowledge the work of the Partnership for 21st Century Skills.
Please visit *www.p21.org* for more information.

Printed in the United States of America
Corporate Graphics

CONTENTS

Water wheels in the city of Hama were once used to bring water to people and to farms.

Struggling Syria

Syria is in southwestern Asia. It is surrounded by Turkey, Jordan, Israel, Iraq, and Lebanon. Syria is about the size of the the state of Washington.

The capital of Syria is Damascus. The country has high mountains, dry deserts, and rich plains.

Some 18 million people live in Syria. However, millions have **emigrated** over the past few years. In 2016, more than 12,000 **refugees** came to the United States. They mainly went to Michigan and California.

The war in Syria has kept many children from going to school.

Tasharafat Bimuqabalatik

Syrians speak Arabic. *Tasharafat Bimuqabalatik* means "Nice to meet you." Written in Arabic, it looks like this:

تشرفت بمقابلتك

The words are written right to left. Numbers, however, are written left to right, as in the United States.

There are more than a dozen Arabic **dialects**. You hear them as you travel from one city to the next. In the east, you might

Parts of Aleppo, Syria's second-largest city, were destroyed during the Syrian Civil War. People are trying to rebuild.

also hear a language called Kurdish. In villages north of Damascus, many people speak Aramaic. It is one of the oldest languages in the world. Syria's largest cities are Aleppo and Damascus. People have lived in these cities since ancient times. People also speak French and English there.

Ask Questions!

Does anyone in your family speak more than one language? If so, how often? Do you have relatives who live in other parts of the country? Do they have a different dialect than you do? Ask your family where they came from. Is there a language in your family's history that you did not know about?

The Quran is an important Islamic book. Muslims believe it contains the words of God, also known as Allah.

Sunni, Shia, and Kurds

Most Syrians are Muslims. They follow the religion of Islam. However, within their faith, they are divided. Most Syrian Muslims are Sunni Muslims. A small number of Syrian Muslims are Shia Muslims, or Shi'ites. There are far more Sunnis in Syria. But the country has been controlled by Shias for more than 45 years. Syria's president is also a Shia Muslim. The two groups fight often.

Kurdish people live in other parts of the Middle East too.

They disagree about who should have become the Muslim community's leader in 632 CE.

Less than 10 percent of Syrians are Kurds. Kurdish people are an **ethnic** group. The Kurds believe in women's rights. They believe in keeping religion and government separate. The majority of Kurds are Sunni Muslims.

Syrian households serve large portions of mezze.
They want their guests to feel welcome.

Kibbeh and *Mezze*

A typical Syrian meal is made up of many small dishes of different foods. This style is known as *mezze*. Everything is meant to be tasted over the course of an hour or more. Try the spicy pepper and walnut dip made with pomegranate molasses. Sample the eggplant-based *baba ghanouj* or the chickpea *hummus*. Taste a serving of *fattoush*. It's a mix of cucumber, radish, tomato, and herbs. Silverware is rarely used. Instead, people

Kibbeh nayyeh is a beloved dish. It is kibbeh served raw.

use pieces of flat bread and lettuce leaves for scooping.

The country's national dish is *kibbeh*. You put bulgur wheat and minced onions in a bowl. Add meat like ground beef, lamb, goat, or camel. Mix in spices like cinnamon, nutmeg, allspice, and cloves. Form the mixture into round balls or flat patties. Then you fry them! These make a tasty side dish or snack.

Create!

Imagine creating a mezze-style dinner. How would you do it? What items would you put in bowls? There would be no main dish. So how would you make sure there was enough to eat? What could you do to help the meal last for an hour?

Syrian citizens protested for more freedom.
They wanted the government to change.

An Ongoing War

Between 2006 and 2010, Syria suffered one of the worst **droughts** in history. Many experts believe that this was the first of many problems for the country. The problems added up. People became desperate for water. Millions of farmers left their fields and moved into the cities. But far too many people lived in these places. There were more people than jobs. They couldn't find

As of December 2017, 5.4 million people have fled Syria.

work. Syrians became unhappy with the government's lack of help and guidance. Protests blossomed into riots. Soon, a civil war erupted. That war continues today. Its violence has chased millions of people out of the country and to safer places. Many escaped to Turkey, Lebanon, and Jordan. No one is sure when they will be able to go home again. But they remain hopeful.

GLOSSARY

dialects (DYE-uh-lekts) ways of speaking in particular areas

droughts (DROUTS) long periods with little or no rain

emigrated (EM-ih-gray-ted) left one country to live in another

ethnic (ETH-nik) of or having to do with a group of people sharing the same national origins, language, or culture

refugees (ref-yoo-JEEZ) people seeking a safe place to live

Syrian Words

baba ghanouj (BAH-bah gah-NOOJ) a dish of cooked eggplant mixed with sesame paste, olive oil, and seasonings

fattoush (fuh-TOUSH) salad made with cucumber, radish, tomato, and herbs

hummus (HUH-muss) a dip or sandwich spread made of chickpeas and sesame paste

kibbeh (kih-BEH) round or flat fried meat patties made with bulgur wheat, minced onions, meat, and spices

mezze (meh-ZAY) a meal made up of many small dishes of all types of food

Tasharafat Bimuqabalatick
(TESH-hah-rah-fah BEE-moo-kah-bah-lah-teek) Nice to meet you

FIND OUT MORE

BOOKS

Gratz, Alan. *Refugee.* New York: Scholastic Press, 2017.

Mason, Helen. *A Refugee's Journey from Syria.* St. Catharines, ON: Crabtree Publishing Company, 2017.

Ruurs, Margriet, and Nizar Ali Badr (illust.). *Stepping Stones: A Refugee Family's Journey.* Victoria, BC: Orca Book Publishers, 2016.

WEBSITES

Ducksters—Syria
www.ducksters.com/geography/country.php?country=Syria
Check out this website to learn the history, geography, and other facts about Syria.

Easy Science for Kids—Syria
http://easyscienceforkids.com/all-about-syria/
Learn about Syria and watch a video showing what life is like in Syria.

INDEX

ABOUT THE AUTHOR

Tamra Orr is the author of hundreds of books for readers of all ages. She graduated from Ball State University, but moved with her husband and four children to Oregon in 2001. She is a full-time author, and when she isn't researching and writing books, she writes letters to friends all over the world. Orr enjoys life in the big city of Portland and feels very lucky to be surrounded by so much diversity.